More Proofreading Practice, Please!

Grade 5

by Dan Greenberg

SCHOLASTIC
PROFESSIONAL BOOKS

New York • Toronto • London • Auckland • Sydney
Mexico City • New Delhi • Hong Kong • Buenos Aires

Cover design by Gerard Fuchs
Cover illustration by Larry Jones
Interior design by Creative Pages, Inc.
Interior illustrations by Mike Moran

ISBN 0-439-18841-5

Contents

Introduction 4
Proofreading Symbols 6

Proofreading for Spelling Errors
Superheroes You've Never Heard Of 7
Money: It's Better Than Ever! 8
Is Nothing Funny? 9
Official Fan Club News for Matt Head, Professional Wrestler 10
Stories Behind Inventions That Changed the World 11
Celebrity Auction 12
The World's Dullest Videos 13
If I Had Three Wishes, Here's What I'd Do 14
How to Get Rid of Common Yard Pests 15

Proofreading for Punctuation and Capitalization Errors
My Most Embarrassing Moment 16
The Really Loud Noise Show 17
Left Brain/Right Brain 18
Teen Beat Magazine Interview: The Four Whiners 19
FAQ.com 20
The Case of the Mummy's Gold 21
Beach Teens 22
Weird Spell 2002 23
Classic Warning Labels 24

Proofreading for Grammar Errors
Danny the K, Proofreader for the Stars 25
Pensington-400 Toasting System 26
The Pegwegger Fashion Collection 27
The Secrets of the Great Decepto 28
What They Do on Their Days Off 29
The Boy Who Cried "Wulf!" 30
True Confessions: I Abandoned My Children! 31
Behind the Special Effects in Today's Hit Movies 32
Jenny Bosco, Olympic Swimmer, and Her Cat Ruffles 33

Proofreading for Mixed Errors
Are You Jealous? 34
A Statement From Class President Mona Turpin 35
Ask Dr. Science 36
Wrong Number! 37
Great Sports Records: The Tanya Macarena Story 38
Dan's Fables: The Donkey and the Dog 39
Dan's Fables: The Dog and the Donkey 40
Great Sports Records: The Benny Bragan Story 41
Can a Horse be Elected President of the United States? 42

Answer Key 43

Introduction

Do you need a book that helps students master the skills of proofreading? To find out if you are ready for *More Proofreading Practice, Please!* take this handy quiz:

1. My students typically proofread their work

   Ⓐ sometimes

   Ⓑ only on weekends

   Ⓒ when pigs have wings

   Ⓓ Are you kidding?

2. Proofreading is an important part of the writing process and provides students with

   Ⓐ 12 vitamins and minerals

   Ⓑ a whole new outlook on the world

   Ⓒ an excuse for why their writing needs help

   Ⓓ Are you kidding?

3. A proofreading error was the cause of

   Ⓐ the War of 1812

   Ⓑ the stock market crash of 1929

   Ⓒ reality TV

   Ⓓ Are you kidding?

Scoring

If you answered D. *Are you kidding?* to all of the above, you're ready for *More Proofreading Practice, Please!* In fact, if you didn't answer *D* above, you're also ready for the book. In general, you need *More Proofreading Practice, Please!* if:

- your students have never heard of proofreading.

- your students have heard of proofreading, but would rather shovel out horse stables with a grapefruit spoon than take the time to proofread their work.

- your students prefer stories, poems, articles, and essays that are engaging, fun, and delightful rather than tedious, dull, and pointless.

- your students like to laugh while they're learning and learn while they're laughing.

- your students need to practice proofreading and editing skills that include punctuation, capitalization, spelling, and grammar skills.

Scholastic Professional Books *More Proofreading Practice, Please! Grade 5*

How to Use This Book

The book is organized into four proofreading subject areas: Spelling, Punctuation and Capitalization, Grammar, and Mixed Errors. Each section includes nine activities.

The Spelling section includes topics such as plurals and homophones. Within the Punctuation and Capitalization section, topics such as proper nouns, possessives, contractions, and comma usage are covered. The Grammar section covers subject-verb agreement, tenses, sentence fragments, and more. The final section invites students to make corrections in all major categories, testing their mastery of proofreading rules.

Selections—in the form of stories, essays, poems, ads, forms, brochures, editorials, diaries, and so on—are presented in a way that allows students to make proofreading corrections right on the page using proofreading symbols. (A reproducible page of common proofreading symbols is provided on page 6.) Be sure to go over how to use these symbols. Annotated answers to each exercise are given at the end of the book.

Classroom Management

Selections in this book can be:

- distributed and completed on an individual basis.

- done as a class with you eliciting volunteer responses.

- assigned as work for partners or small cooperative groups to complete.

- distributed for homework or in-class work.

- completed as part of a Writing Program or Writing Lab.

- incorporated as part of a Five-Step Writing Process program that includes Prewriting, Drafting, Revising, Proofreading, and Publishing.

You might also try:

- having students trade writing samples and proofread each other's work.

- having students proofread papers that they have written for other subjects, such as social studies, science, or math.

- playing a proofreading game in which students are challenged to find, for example, "all 27 errors in this article."

Going Beyond

The true test of proofreading exercises is whether they carry over into students' own writing. To find out, ask students to write their own selections (based on selections in this book!) and proofread them. Stress that proofreading should include not only correcting errors, but also paying attention to the content and structure of the writing and making sure that all ideas are expressed as clearly and succinctly as possible.

Most of All

Try to make proofreading a fun part of the writing process that students look forward to doing, rather than a chore that hangs over their heads. Point out that the selections in this book become clearer, and thus more interesting, engaging, and *funny* only after they are proofread and minor errors are eliminated.

Proofreading Symbols

a ~~tiny~~ kitten   ⌐ Delete (Take it away forever!)

sleep all ~~day~~ ^{night}   ⌐ Delete and change to something else

¶ It was a dark and stormy night.   ¶ Begin a new paragraph

ⓛⒸ A Horse's mane   ⓛⒸ Lowercase that capital letter

ⒸⒶⓅ in Santa Fe, New mexico   ⒸⒶⓅ Capitalize that lowercase letter

Cheyenne Wyoming   ⌄ Insert comma

Carlos asked, "How are you?"   ⌄ ⌄ Insert quotation marks

An ant ambled about   ⊙ Insert period

Where is Copenhagen?   ? Insert question mark

A cat slipped on the floor waxed.   ∿ Transpose (or trade positions)

Scholastic Professional Books More Proofreading Practice, Please! Grade 5

Name _____ Date _____

Superheroes You've Never Heard Of

Find and mark the ten spelling errors.

Pizza-Eating Girl

She can eat pizza with anything on it—
anything! You want ice cream and
raisens on your pizza? She can eat
it! How about a pizza with
lemon drops and
selery? She can eat it!
Her skills come in
handy when villains
try to force the heroes
to eat unpleasant
pizza combinations.

Dictionary Man

He can look up words in the dictionary faster than any other living human being.
His powwers are useful for fighting aginst villains who use really big words.

Worm Woman

She lives underground. She can comunecate with worms; not that worms have
much to say. She often ends up stuck on the sidewalk in the hot sun after a
rainey day.

Bargain Man

He can buy anything for the lowest possible price. This is especialy helpful when
other superheroes need to buy tites and uniforms. He always finds a bargain!

Gesundheit Woman

With her super hearing, she can hear people sneezeing miles away. Her powers
come in handy when bad guys are hideing in corners and they sneeze.

Name _____ Date _____

Money: It's Better Than Ever!

Find and mark the ten spelling errors.

The U.S. Mint makes money every day. Did you know that today's money is better then ever? To see why, keep reading.

Money is 100% all naturle! That's right. There are no artificial ingreedients in U.S. money. Your dollars are as pure and naturle as a tall redwood tree!

Money goes everywhere! Going to the beach? Take some money. Taking a vacashun? Try taking money with you. Making a busyness deal? You'll find that money comes in handy!

Money comes in great sizes and stiles! Do you like paper money or coins? Big amounts or small? Green or sliver? No matter what your needs, we've got the money for you. In the styles and sizes that fit your active lifestyle.

Money has lots of uses! Want to buy something? Buy it with money. You can buy almost anything with money, including shoelaces, cinnimon rolls, hairbrushs, and even Super Bowl tickets (if you can get them).

Scholastic Professional Books *More Proofreading Practice, Please! Grade 5*

Name _____ Date _____

Is Nothing Funny?

Find and mark the ten spelling errors.

"On the subject of humor and comedy,"
Said Professor Mary Francis Pfaff,
"Nothing can ever be *proven* to be funny
So there's no real reasin to lagh!"

"Laughter has no real purrposs,"
Said the famous doctor of grins.
"It's just a nervous habit we have
Like fish that wiggle their fins."

"The data is clear," the professor said.
"In my research, I've fownd
There's just no point in opening your mowth
And making a 'Ha ha!' sound."

Just then a tiny inchworm
Hanging by its miniature toes
Dropped down from the sealing above
Rite on the tip of my nose!

When the professor seemed to chukle,
I said, "Excuse me, Professer Pfaff,
Didn't you say that *nothing's* funny?
There's *never* a reason to laugh?"

"Well," replied the professor.
"I'll admit one thing is true.
It *can* be funny when an inchworm lands—
At leest when it lands on you!"

Scholastic Professional Books *More Proofreading Practice, Please! Grade 5*

9

Name _____ Date _____

Official Fan Club News for Matt Head, Professional Wrestler

Find and mark the ten spelling errors.

Keeping Track of Matt

Tho he had no wrestling matches this week, Matt Head was very busy. These are some of the things he accomplished this week.

- He drouled.
- He got into an arguenent with a tree.
- He put his tights on backwords.

Fan Club Poll

We asked you to answer the question: *What does Matt Head remind you of most?* Here are the rezults.

- A floor mat—14%
- A big head without a brane—62%
- A wrestling mat with no brains who argues with trees—24%

Matt Head's Diet Plan

- Breakfast: 14-ounce box of corn flakes, including the box, and 2 gallones of milk
- Light Lunch: pasta, salad, and metel screws
- Power Dinner: raw leather with radiator fluid sause

Contest Results

Here are the results of our contest, "Why I don't want to spend the day with Matt Head." We only receved one entry. Here it is.

I don't want to spend the day with Matt Head. I certainly hope I don't win this contest. —Jason Dorf

Scholastic Professional Books *More Proofreading Practice, Please! Grade 5*

Name _____ Date _____

Stories Behind Inventions That Changed the World

(That May or May Not Be True)

Find and mark the ten spelling errors.

The Jacket Zipper

The first zipper, the Model 100-A, was made of solid wood and weyed over 17 ponds. Over time, the size decreased. Metal replased wood. A solid gold zipper weighed in at only 4.1 ownces. Unfortunatelly, it cost over $1,500. Finally, the Model 100-Z came out. It was a lot like the zipper of today—except two people were required to zip it up.

The Bookmark

Ted E. Bear, in a 1997 interview, discloseed, "I kept loosing my place in the book I was reading. I tried putting a peece of cheese in there, but it was greasy. I tried a giant rock. It was too heavy and awkward. I tried a $100 bill. It worked well, but that was all the money I had! Finally, I tried a small slip of paper. At last, the bookmark was born!"

The Cereal Spoon

First, people tried to eat cereal with their hands. What a mess! There was milk driping from everyone's elbows. Next, a garden shovel was tried. Too big! It was replaced with a fork. The size was good, but it leaked. Finally, someone pulled out a spoon. There was little chance after so many faillurs that it would work. But, it was perfect!

Scholastic Professional Books *More Proofreading Practice, Please! Grade 5*

11

Name _____ Date _____

Celebrity Auction

Find and mark the ten spelling errors.

These items will be offerred at the Annual Celebrity Auction.

Item #406B: Hair clippings from country singer Milt Hayseed

Milt gets a harecut every week. His barber collects the clippings. Bidding starts at $50 a bunch. Each bunch contains fourty or more strands.

Item #418C: Peanut butter sandwich not eaten by child superstar Spencer Twirp

When Spencer was on his cross-country tour, one of his assistants ordered a sandwhich for him. "I hate peanut butter!" cried Spencer. This is the very sandwich that Spencer never touched. Bidding starts at $1,200.

Item #423A: Elevator button pushed by movie souperstar Tanya Ruffage

When Tanya made the classic film *Dripless*, she stayed on the eleventh flour of the Park Boulevard Hotle. This is the elevator button she pushed to get to that flore. Bidding starts at $13,000.

Item #511D: Towel used by sports star Manny Meshooga

During the 2002 semi-finals, a fan gave Manny this towel to autograph. Manny didn't sine it, but he did wipe his shoes on the towell. Bidding starts at $5,000.

Scholastic Professional Books *More Proofreading Practice, Please! Grade 5*

Name _____ Date _____

The World's Dullest Videos

Find and mark the ten spelling errors.

Do you love dull videos? Then this is the collection for you. For only $39.95 per month we'll delivver a video to your door. The selecttins include these titels.

Water Boiling

This classic shows the entire process, from stert to finnish. Watch as the pot is filled with water. See the heat being turned on! Then wait for the water to bole. It seems like it takes forrever!

Grass Growing

Are you an outdoor-type person? Do you love nature? This fabulous 24-part video is for you. Watch as, at first, nothing seems to happen. But then as the ours (and days!) pass, a change occurs. Isn't the grass a tiny bit longer than it was at the begining? Watch for the sequel, *Mowing*.

The Stone

This is the video for true rock fans. No scenery. No talk. No music. Just a camera focused on a common stone for six solid hours. Nothing happens. Nothing changes. By far, this is the dulest video in our collection!

Name _____ Date _____

If I Had Three Wishes, Here's What I'd Do

Find and mark the ten spelling errors.

If I had three wishs, here's what I'd do:

I'd use my first wish (which would leaf me just too)

And wish for three wishes—that would make five,

Which would make me the luckyest person alive!

Because after that, I could wish again,

And keep on going until I'd passt ten.

Then I'd keep wishing until I had a bunch,

Then I'd stop, take a brake, and wish for something good for lunch.

After lunch I'd wish more and pile up the wishes—

Elleven, twelve, but not thurteen (you see, I'm superstitious).

After I had a hunderd wishes, I think I'd take a break.

I wouldn't want to get tired and make a foolish mistake.

If I had a *thousand* wishes, maybe that'd be enough,

Or maybe I'd keep going, and wish for yet more stuff.

After a *million* wishes, I guess I'd need no more.

So then I'd start wishing for ideaes of things

To use my million wishes for.

Scholastic Professional Books *More Proofreading Practice, Please! Grade 5*

Name _____ Date _____

How to Get Rid of Common Yard Pests

Find and mark the ten spelling errors.

Michael, the five-year-old pest who trampels your rose bushes

Young children are drawn to the sound of bells. Get a bell that sounds just like the one on your lockal ice cream truck. Go arond to the front of the house and ring the bell. Close the gate after he leaves.

Ms. Peeve, the door-to-door salesperson

Tell Ms. Peeve that you can't talk right now. But you'd like to talk latter by telephone. Ask for Ms. Peeve's home phone number. This should friten her away for good.

Steve, the teenage pest

Teenaegers don't like corny music. Get a recording of some really lame music. Turn the vollume up louwd. This should get rid of Steve in no time.

Bonnie, the cat who hides under your porch

Cats are drawn to the sound of a can opening. Go out in the front yard, well away from the affectted area. Open a can of something that cats don't like, like spinech or green beans. Bonnie will come running. But she'll be so disappointed that she won't come back again.

Scholastic Professional Books More Proofreading Practice, Please! Grade 5

15

Name _____ Date _____

My Most Embarrassing Moment
by Lulu the Spider

Find and mark the ten punctuation and capitalization errors.

This is *so* embarrassing that I can barely talk about it. Let me start by telling you a little bit about myself. I'm a spider. My name is Lulu. I live in a web that I spin each and every day. It's in the attic of a building on eighth street. I picked this location because I have Eight legs.

I eat insects. That may sound yucky to you. I think they are delicious.

One more thing I've got poisonous fangs. I could bring down an elephant if I needed to: but I prefer insects.

This is my embarrassing moment. I was sitting in my web in the attic of 1818 Eighth Street, Hartford connecticut. I heard a rustling. "Aha!" I thought. "Lunch!

I heard some struggling and a muffled cry for help. So I rushed over to the noise. I wrapped the victim up in silk. I was just about to inject my poison when I heard a voice cry. "It's me! Walter!"

"Walter?" I thought. It wasn't an insect at all. It was an arachnid, like me. In fact, it was Walter the Spider, my boyfriend! I had caught him in my web! I had even wrapped him up.

I was so embarrassed I thought I'd never live it down. Walter forgave me and we played on swings made of silk that Walter hung from my Web.

Scholastic Professional Books *More Proofreading Practice, Please! Grade 5*

Name _____ Date _____

The Really Loud Noise Show

Find and mark the ten punctuation and capitalization errors.

Good Evening; I'm Bob Drumm. Welcome to "the Really Loud Noise Show." Each week on "The Really Loud Noise Show", we bring you the loudest noise we can find. We'll start off today with a really loud train going 80 miles per hour.

Next, we add, the trains whistle.

We follow the train noises with the noon ringing of bells in a nearby church.

The next thing you hear will be the sound heard if you were parked across the street from the church in a car with huge stereo speakers blaring loud music while your passenger is beating a garbage can with a hammer. Meanwhile a dog is sitting in the backseat and is barking furiously at a Mail Carrier who is passing by.

For our final loud noise of the evening, the railroad tracks are next to a school playground where one hundred screaming kindergarten students have just started to play. Of course, an Ice cream truck has just pulled up.

Now that's some loud noise! See you next week, everyone! What? You can't hear me? I'd better speak *louder*!

Scholastic Professional Books *More Proofreading Practice, Please! Grade 5*

17

Name _____ Date _____

Left Brain/Right Brain

Find and mark the ten punctuation and capitalization errors.

Your brain has a left side and a right side. Each side is specialized for different tasks.

Your left brain is good for arguing, counting money, thinking of excuses making hasty decisions, changing TV channels, and thinking of someone to blame when something goes wrong.

Your right brain is good for arranging furniture; jumping to conclusions, getting mad when something goes wrong finding lost socks, and remembering where things are in the refrigerator.

How do your two brains work together to solve a problem? Read the following problem to find out.

Two trains leave their stations at exactly 12 noon. One is traveling at 80 miles per hour from Baltimore to Pittsburgh. The other is traveling at 63 miles per hour from Pittsburgh to baltimore. How much is the lunch special on the second train.

Your left brain springs into action first, thinking, "I could'nt solve this problem in a million years.

Then your right brain contributes "I can't solve this problem either."

Now your left brain takes control, thinking, "I give up. There's no point in trying?"

Finally your right brain finishes the task, "I'm hungry. I'll make a peanut butter sandwich."

Scholastic Professional Books *More Proofreading Practice, Please! Grade 5*

Name _____ Date _____

Teen Beat Magazine Interview:
The Four Whiners

Find and mark the ten punctuation and capitalization errors.

TEEN BEAT: Welcome. We're interviewing this months' hottest new band—The Four whiners.

WHINERS: Hi.

TEEN BEAT: Why don't you introduce yourselves.

GUMBY: I'm Gumby Carlson. I do the lead lip-synching.

WEASEL: I'm Weasel Whitney. I just stand on stage.

CINDY: I'm Cindy Cruz from a Ranch in Montana. I make my lips pout. See?

MONICA: I'm Monica Silver. I hum. Then everyone always tells me to be quiet.

TEEN BEAT: Tell us about your new CD called The Cheese songs."

GUMBY: We haven't really heard it yet.

TEEN BEAT: Don't you know what's on it?

CINDY: You have to understand. First, real Musicians play the music.

WEASEL: Then good singers sing the songs.

MONICA: Then dancers are filmed for the videos.

TEEN BEAT: What do you four actually do.

WEASEL: We sort of hang around backstage and play card games.

TEEN BEAT: Is it true that, except for your photograph on the cover, you really had no part in the making of your own hit CD?

GUMBY: *(taking off his mask)* Actually, we wear masks.

TEEN BEAT: *(shocked)* Oh, my goodness.

MONICA: *(shrugs)* Would you like our autographs!

Scholastic Professional Books *More Proofreading Practice, Please! Grade 5*

19

Name _____ Date _____

FAQ.com

Find and mark the ten punctuation and capitalization errors.

Welcome, to FAQ.com. FAQ stands for Frequently Asked Questions. FAQ.com attempts to answer questions about those Questions.

QUESTION What's your most frequently asked question?

ANSWER The most frequently asked question is, "What is your most frequently asked question"?

QUESTION Isn't that what I just asked?

ANSWER No, you asked, "*What's* your most frequently asked question?" We answered "The most frequently asked question is, 'What *is* your most frequently asked question?'"

QUESTION Why am I so confused.

ANSWER That's the second-most frequently, asked question. The answer is, "Because the answer to your first question was so confusing, you're still confused.

QUESTION So what should I do?

ANSWER We suggest that you go to Confused.com. This, site gives answers to people who have become confused after visiting Our site. Good Luck.

Home   **About Us**   **Contact Us**   **Still Confused?**

Scholastic Professional Books *More Proofreading Practice, Please! Grade 5*

Name _____ Date _____

The Case of the Mummy's Gold

Find and mark the ten punctuation and capitalization errors.

Hello, I'm Lucy Luck. I'm a private eye. I was sitting in my office when Dr. Jane Hanks, the famous Explorer, walked in. A couple of years ago Dr. Hanks found the famous Mummy's Gold. However, the gold had been stolen from her and she'd been searching for it ever since.

"Look at this letter," Dr. Hanks said. The letter contained a map of what looked like the Gobi desert. "I traveled to Mongolia in asia and searched everywhere in the southeast corner of the Gobi Desert. I didn't find the Gold."

"Are you hungry, Dr. Hanks? I asked. "Let's go eat dinner."

I took her to a dark and distant neighborhood. We walked into a little restaurant called gobi's.

"Surely," she said, "you don't think—"

I went to a small table in the southeast corner of the restaurant. A sign said, "Dessert." I looked under the table. There was a large chest filled with the Mummy's Gold!

"You found it!" cried Dr. Hanks "How, can I ever thank you?"

"It's no big deal," I said, even though I knew it was.

"I just have one question," said Dr. Hanks as we hauled the chest out. "I looked at the map. It says *Desert*, not *Dessert*. It's clear as a bell."

"Hey," I said. "People make mistakes."

"They sure do?" said Dr. Hanks.

Name _____ Date _____

Beach Teens

This week's episode: "The Thanksgiving Dance"

Find and mark the ten punctuation and capitalization errors.

The following is the script for the new hit TV show starring Jason Goozle and Jennie Fibb.

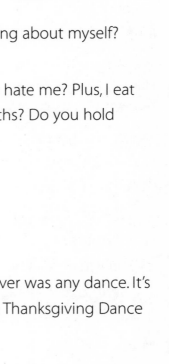

Jennie: Jason I can't go with you to the Thanksgiving Dance.

Jason: Why not? Is it because I'm dull unpopular, and have a bad haircut.

Jennie: No, it's not that.

Jason: Is it because I'm rude, I mumble, and I never Stop talking about myself?

Jennie: No, it's not that, either.

Jason: Then what is it Jennie? Is it because all of your friends hate me? Plus, I eat dog food? And I haven't taken a bath in over six months? Do you hold those things against me, Jennie?

Jennie: No, Jason, I don't. I don't know how to say this?

Jason: Go ahead and say it, Jennie. I can take it.

Jennie: There's not going to be a, Thanksgiving Dance, Jason.

Jason: Was it cancelled?

Jennie: No, it wasn't cancelled. There isn't any dance. There never was any dance. It's not even Thanksgiving, Jason. It's july. You can't have a Thanksgiving Dance in July.

Jason: So, does that mean you won't be going with me?

Jennie: No I won't.

Jason: One more thing, Jennie. Suppose it were Thanksgiving, and suppose there were a Thanksgiving Dance. Would you have gone with me?

Jennie: Not a chance, Jason.

Jason: I, thought so.

Scholastic Professional Books *More Proofreading Practice, Please! Grade 5*

Name _____ Date _____

Weird Spell 2002

Find and mark the ten punctuation and capitalization errors.

Juan: Welcome to "Weird Spell 2002." It's the game where Players compete to see who can spell words in the weirdest way. I'm Juan Bost, your host. And now, let's hear from our first weird speller.

Donna: My name is Donna pike. I'm a really weird speller. One time I spelled *cat* without a *c*, an *a*, or a *t*!

Juan: Wow! Here's your first word, Donna. Spell *fishes*.

Moozik; Skule

Donna: That would be "*p-h-i-c-i-o-u-s*."

Kumpoott~her

Juan: That's really weird, Donna. How do you explain it!

Donna: The *ph* makes an "F" sound in the word *phonograph*.

Juan: Oh that's clever.

Donna: Then the end of the word is just like the end of *Suspicious*.

Juan: That's clever, Donna. That sure is a weird way to spell a Word.

Donna: Thank, you very much. What do I win?

Juan: You win a million dollars! sorry, did I say "million"? I meant to say, "you win the *ten*-dollar prize!"

Uhmaze-Zing

Donna: Well, thanks anyway

Juan: That's all the time we have now for "Weird Spell 2002"—the game where players spell words in weird ways.

Name _____ Date _____

Classic Warning Labels

Find and mark the ten punctuation and capitalization errors.

Warning on Shoes

The soles on these shoes are made of Rubber. In the event that you are attacked by a group of rubber-eating space aliens, take off shoes. Do *not* leave a trail of erasers for them to follow!

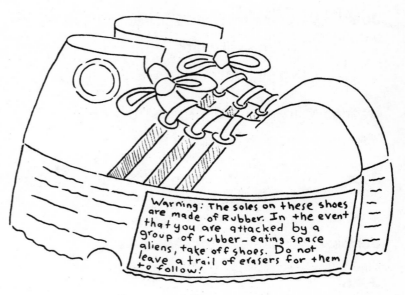

Warning on Alligator Exhibit

Please refrain from jumping over the fence swimming the moat scaling the wall, and poking the alligators with a stick. Do not say;"You can't hurt me a bit!" Alligators *can* hurt you a bit.

Warning on Movie Poster

This film is rated E P. (Extremely Pointless). please do not try to analyze the plot, understand the characters, or figure out what happens in the end. For the most part, this movie does not make any sense?

Warning on Tomato Sauce Can

Tomato sauce is not intended to be poured on cornflakes in hair, or in fish bowls. People who pour it in their hair may develop symptoms of Tomato Sauce hair Condition. This condition includes hair that smells like tomato sauce and that could be eaten if somebody is foolish enough, to try it.

Scholastic Professional Books *More Proofreading Practice, Please! Grade 5*

Name _____ Date _____

Danny the K, Proofreader for the Stars

Find and mark the ten grammar errors.

My name is Danny the K. I don't like to brag, but I'll probably the greatest proofreader of all time. I've proofread for presidents, kings, pop stars, quarterbacks, and movie tycoons.

I'll never forget the day the president call me up. "Danny," he said. "You got to proofread my speech. I'll gave you the Medal of Honor. I'll name a street after you. Just tell me what you want. I'll do it."

"Hold on a second, Mr. President," I say. "I don't want a Medal of Honor. I don't want a street. I'm just a proofreader. I just want to do my job."

"You am right," said the president. "I'm sorry."

I proofreading the speech for him. Wouldn't you know it? That was the finer speech he ever made!

Then there was the time my favorite actor, Marva Marvelous, called me. "Darling," she said. "You just *must* proofread my new script. If you did, I'll give you *anything*. I'll give you a million dollars."

"Hold on a second there, Marva," I said. "I'm just a proofreader, not a movie star. I can't take a million dollars for that."

"Why not?" Marva asked.

"Because I want *two* million dollars," I said.

Now two million dollars may seem to be a ridiculous amount for someone to pay for proofreading. But, I proofread this piece and you can see what a greatest job I did!

Scholastic Professional Books *More Proofreading Practice, Please! Grade 5*

25

Name _____ Date _____

Pensington-400 Toasting System

Find and mark the ten grammar errors.

Congratulations! You is the proud new owner of the Pensington-400 Toasting System.

Before You Toast

Make sure that you have the proper equipment. You will need the Pensington-400, bread, butters, a knife, safety goggles and helmet, and a plate.

Safety Precautions

Always wore your safety goggles and helmet when using the toaster. When properly handled, toast is 100% safe. Beware of high-speed toast particles that break off from the main bread slice while buttering. These particles can travel at speeds up to 125 mile per hour.

Troubleshooting

Problem: My helmet come unsnapped while I was buttering. What should I do?

Solution: Stopped buttering immediately. With your left hand, stabilize the toast. When you are sure the toast are safe, use your right hand to snap your helmet. Once her helmet is secure, resume buttering.

Problem: I were making toast when I hear sirens. Firefighters broke down my front door. What happened?

Solution: You may have burned your toast. Is it covered with flames? Do the flames reach halfway to the ceiling? If so, then read page 54, "How to survive a burnt toast emergency."

Name _____ Date _____

The Pegwegger Fashion Collection

Find and mark the ten grammar errors.

Marvelous Muffin Mittens

While traveling in a rural area of upper Scotland, I notice the locals wearing marvelous mittens. I said to Roland, my assistant, "You and me need pairs of those mittens." It seems the people were wearing special kinds of muffins shaped like mittens. Now the new Pegwegger Collection offer "Muffin Mittens." Of course, if you get hungry, you can eat your mittens!

Bus Boy Slacks

Have you noticed how great café bus boys look? That's because they spill food on their pants. The "café bus boy look" will inspired fabulous pants. Be cautious, don't wear the pants near hungriest dogs!

Tissue Box Shoes

I were lying by the pool in Pango Pango when I noticed that I'd left my comfortabler shoes inside my hotel room. What was I to do? I taked two tissue boxes and putted them on my feet. Like all great ideas, the Tissue Box Shoes came from this event. Furthermore, I wore the Tissue Box Shoes in a soccer game and score three goals!

Scholastic Professional Books *More Proofreading Practice, Please! Grade 5*

27

Name _____ Date _____

The Secrets of the Great Decepto

Find and mark the ten grammar errors.

The Saw-the-Assistant-in-Half Trick

First, I put my assistant in a box. Next, I wave a curtain over the box. Then, I saw the box in half. Final, I put the two half back together. When my assistant gets up, the audience applauds.

How it's done: When I pull the curtain over the box I run backstage. I were quickly replaced by a real magician who knows how to do the trick. I stand backstage until the trick are over. I run back at the end as the audience applauded.

The Pull-a-Rabbit-Out-of-a-Hat Trick

First, I show the audience a hat. There is nothing inside. Next, I put on the hat. Then, I wave my hand and take off the hat. When a rabbit jumps out, the audience applauds.

How it's done: When I wave my hand, I'm actually giving the signal for a rabbit to run onto the stage. This rabbit is a licensed magician and know how to performs the trick flawlessly. When the trick is over, the audience applauds.

The Float-the-Assistant-Above-the-Stage Illusion

First, my assistant lies down. Next, I pass my cape over her. Then, she begins to float. I pass hoops around her to show that she are not being held by wires. The audience applauds.

How it's done: When I pass my cape over my assistant, a flock of trained hummingbirds flies on the stage and lifts her in the air. They hover in the air while I pass hoops to show that there are no wires. When the hummingbirds left, my assistant stands up and the audience applauded.

Scholastic Professional Books *More Proofreading Practice, Please! Grade 5*

Name _____ Date _____

What They Do on Their Days Off

Find and mark the ten grammar errors.

Centipede

On my day off, I try to stay off my feet. I had one hundred of them, you know. Sometimes my brother and me go shopping for shoes. That's not easy when you each need fifty pairs!

Toll Booth Collector

I loves collecting tolls. I sets up a table on my street. I collect tolls from bigger cars, small trucks, and even children on tricycles. Don't worry, I always give the money back!

Clown

I likes to go shopping for clown equipment. Do you know how hard is it to find clown shoes? Or, has you ever shopped for glow-in-the-dark orange hair? Also, I like to practice squirting people with lapel flowers.

House Fly

I sometime sit on a window blind for about twelve hours and do nothing. Most of the time, I like making a pest of myself. Hey, when you're a fly, that's what you do!

Billionaire

I like to count money. I empty all the change from the pockets of my hundreds of suits. I pulling the coins from my penny loafers. I like to make stacks of coins and bills on my dining room table. My favorite hobby is counting and this gives me a chance to practice it.

Scholastic Professional Books *More Proofreading Practice, Please! Grade 5*

29

Name _____ Date _____

The Boy Who Cried "Wulf!"

Find and mark the ten grammar errors.

There once was a smallest car company named Wulf whose cars were not selling well.

The Big Boss was frustrated. She hire a boy to sit by the road and look at the cars that went by.

"You sit right here," she told the boy. "Every time you saw a Wulf drive by I want you to cry 'Wulf!'"

The boy done as he was told. Each time a Wulf drove by he cried, "Wulf!"

This might have been the end of the story were it not for a real wolf that happened to come by.

The boy cry, "Wolf!" when he saw the real wolf. But, not no one paid any attention.

"I mean it!" he repeated. "It be a wolf!" Again, no one paid any attention.

So when the real wolf come to where the Big Boss was sitting, she and the Wulf sales force panicked and run. The wolf stayed and ate all of the food on the buffet table.

In the end, the boy stayed on the job until many year later when he took over as Big Boss.

The moral of the story is . . .
Never cry wulf *when it's really a wolf!*

Scholastic Professional Books *More Proofreading Practice, Please! Grade 5*

Name _____ Date _____

True Confessions:
I Abandoned My Children!

by Mary Frog

Find and mark the ten grammar errors.

I still can't believe it. I always thought I'd be a good mother, but something come over me. I still don't know what.

I should say a little about myself. I was born in a larger pond. I come from a biggest family. There was 4,000 in my family. That's 2,000 girls and 2,000 boys. We were the bigger family in the pond.

My mother leave us. We were only young tadpoles, but we were on our own. I remember think, *When I have kids, it won't be like this.*

But then, sure enough, I lay about 5,000 eggs. I was determined to treat each and every one of them like an individuals.

Then something came over me. Suddenly, I just hopped up and left. I got on the Internet and looked up frog behavior. No wonder I let my tadpoles go!

Epilog

I was surprised and proud at how good my children all turned out. Thousands made it. They is good croakers. They grew up tall and straight and green. Just like me!

Scholastic Professional Books *More Proofreading Practice, Please! Grade 5*

31

Name _____ Date _____

Behind the Special Effects in Today's Hit Movies

Find and mark the ten grammar errors.

Dear State-of-the-Art,

Recently, I seen the movie *Detonation*, starring Arnold Morphus. It had a lot of great special effect. But, the part I likeded best come near the end. There were not no car chases, and not even any space aliens in the scene. The two characters was just talking. How did they do that?

Signed,

Curious

Dear Curious,

The part of the movie that you liked is called *acting*. Acting requires that the stars act, talk, and make gestures just like real people. Though acting in todays' movies is quite rare, believe it or not, in the olden days, acting was actually quite common in movies!

Signed,

State-of-the-Art

Dear State-of-the-Art,

How did they make the four cockroaches speak its lines in the movie *Roach Motel*?

Signed,

PUZZLED

Dear Puzzled,

This is an easy one! They just hold up cue cards. The roach read their lines right off the cue cards.

Signed,

State-of-the-Art

Scholastic Professional Books *More Proofreading Practice, Please! Grade 5*

Name _____ Date _____

Jenny Bosco, Olympic Swimmer, and Her Cat Ruffles

A Heart-Warming Story

Find and mark the ten grammar errors.

My name is Jenny Bosco. I'm an Olympic swimmer. I swim in the 50-yard free-style dog paddle. I always thought that Ruffles, my best friend, would be there beside me.

On the first day of training, I notice something was wrong. I jump in the pool, but Ruffles didn't follow me.

I took her to seven different specialists. They all came to the same conclusion: *Cats doesn't like water.*

So each day, I would swim laps. Ruffles would sat by the pool reading the newspaper. But, Ruffles seem restless.

Then I heard more bad news. I took Ruffles to the eye doctor. He tell me that *cats can't read.*

Once again, I were crushed. I thought, *I'll won a gold medal in the Olympics anyway.*

Well, I didn't win a gold medal. In fact, I missed the whole competition. On the day of the race, I oversleep and was disqualified. Ruffles'es watch had stopped!

I swam anyway. It was during the *diving* competition. I was almost hit by someone doing a two-and-one-half-full-twisting gainer. But as the police escorted me away, I thought about Ruffles. She may hate water. She may never learn to read. But, she still is my best friend. I think she and I will go out for the three-legged race next Olympics.

Scholastic Professional Books *More Proofreading Practice, Please! Grade 5*

33

Name _____ Date _____

Are You Jealous?

Find and mark the twelve errors. They may be spelling, punctuation, capitalization, or grammar errors.

Bert: Welcome to the quiz show, "Are You Jealous?" I'm Bert Envy, your host. Our first contestunt is Edna Fingers. Edna, here are your first question. *Suppose your best friend Jasper gets a new puppy for his birthday. Are you jealous.*

Edna: No, Bert, I'm not.

Bert: Correct for 50 points! And what's your reson, Edna?

Edna: I has my own puppy, Bert. Plus, my puppy doesn't chew on shoes the way Jasper's puppy does.

Bert: Very nice, Edna, here's your second question. *Suppose Jasper get invited to go over to Scooter's house to play and you don't get to go. Are you jealous?*

Edna: No, I'm not, Bert. I'll tell you why. I don't like to go over to Scooter's and play with his Video games. I'd rather stay here by myself.

Bert: And that is correct for 100 points! Now here's your final question, Edna. *Your friend Jasper gets to be on the TV show "Who wants a Sandwich?" Are you jealous?*

Edna: No, I'm not Bert, because I'm currently appearing on a TV show.

Bert: "Who Wants a Sandwitch?" is a more popular show than "Are You Jealous?" So, you're *incorrect*, Edna. You *should* be jealous. That's mynus 150 points! Which brings your score to zero, goose egg, nothing.

Edna: Bye, Bert. I'm going to try out for "Who Wants a Sandwich?"

Bert: That's all the time we has now. See you next time?

Scholastic Professional Books *More Proofreading Practice, Please! Grade 5*

Name _____ Date _____

A Statement From
Class President Mona Turpin

Find and mark the twelve errors. They may be spelling, punctuation, capitalization, or grammar errors.

My fellow Classmates, as pressident of our class, I know that you have put your trust in me. You trusted me when you elected me president. You trusted me when we passed the recess rule that increased the length of recess by over 15 purcent. You trusted me when I asked for their support on the candy ban.

At that time; I explained how I felt. Candy is bad for you. It rot your teeth. It's expensive. Basically, it has no place in our school.

When we passed the candy ban, I felt proud. I felt we had done something for all of the students of webster School. I still feel that way.

Recently though, some trubbling events have come to light. Candy wrappers were found in my locker. My book bag was described as "smelling like chocolate.

I'd *like* to tell you that these accusations are a mistake. I'd *like* to say that I didn't bring candy to school. I'd *like* to say that I didn't eat it secretly in the Student Council Room, stuffing it into my mouth as fast as I could.

But if I told you these things, I'd be lying. All I can tell you is that I am sorry. What did I learn from this experiense? I learned about honesty. I learned about responsibility. I learned that it's easier to talk the talk than to walk the walk. I learned all of these things. But most of all, I learnt something about myself.

I learned that I *really* like candy.

Scholastic Professional Books *More Proofreading Practice, Please! Grade 5*

35

Name _____ Date _____

Ask Dr. Science

Questions for a Scientist Who Knows Just About Everything!

Find and mark the twelve errors. They may be spelling, punctuation, capitalization, or grammar errors.

Question: How do we know that Earth goes around the sun?

Dr. Science: It's obvious that Earth goes airound something. Is it a Telephone pole? Is it a raccoon? If you look closely in a science book you will see a digram with a Tiny Earth traveling around the sun—not around a telephone pole or a raccoon?

Question: What are photosynthesis?

Dr. Science: Photosynthesis is what happens when someone is taking a picture and you look the other way. Then you get the photograph back and you look really stupid. Then you say, "Photosynthesis caused that to happen."

Question: How do a cumputer work?

Dr. Science: There is three ways to make a computer work. First, plug it in. Second turn it on. And third, say out lowd, "Why won't this thing work?"

Question: Why do birds fly south?

Dr. Science: Birds are looking for coins on the ground. They fly a little bit. Then they fly a little bit more. Pretty soon, they ends up in Florida.

Scholastic Professional Books *More Proofreading Practice, Please!* Grade 5

Name _____ Date _____

Wrong Number!

Find and mark the twelve errors. They may be spelling, punctuation, capitalization, or grammar errors.

The following is some of the most outrageously rong numbers ever dialed. This first call came to the house of Mr. Rudy Remo of Baltimore, maryland. Listen closerly.

Caller: Hello, who's this?

Rudy: No who is this?

Caller: I was trying to call 555-3221.

Rudy: This is 555-9928. You're not even close!

Caller: Wow! You're right. I'm sorry. I really am.

Rudy: That's okay. It could happen to anyone.

But *could* it happen to anyone? Listen to what happens next at the Remo household.

Caller: Hello, is Erica there?

Rudy: There is not no Erica here. What number were you trying to reach?

Caller: I am trying to reach 555-3221.

Rudy: Well, your off by a mile. This is 555-9928. Say, didn't you just call a few minutes ago?

Caller: *(disguising his voice)* Who, I? No, it must have been someone else.

There you have it—a number so wrong that we have our esperts analyze the last four digits. Do you know what they found! Every digit was wrong! Not a single digit was correct! Now, how's that for a shocking event?

Scholastic Professional Books *More Proofreading Practice, Please! Grade 5*

37

Name _____ Date _____

Great Sports Records:
The Tanya Macarena Story

Find and mark the twelve errors. They may be spelling, punctuation, capitalization, or grammar errors.

"Winning a match is great," said tennis legend Tanya Macarena. "But do you know what's more important than winning? What I wear on the court. That's what it's really all about."

It wasn't always like this for Tanya Macarena. At one point she was satisfyed just winning matches. And, as the Top player in the world, she won a lot of matches.

"But something were missing," revealed Tanya. "I would win my match, but then I would look over and see that my opponents outfit was silliest than mine. This bothered me."

So Tanya hired Minnie Vulch to desin her tennis outfits.

Ms. Vulch said, "I don't know nothing about fashtion. You'll be able to tell by my designs."

Over time; Ms. Vulch helped design dozens of new outfits for Tanya. Each one was silly than the last.

"At first, my outfits were silly, but not really ridiculous," said Tanya. "The real breakthrough came at the U.s. Open. I wore what can be discribed as a clown suit."

"I was amazed she could play with those big floppy shoes and the red rubber nose," confessed Minnie.

But Tanya not only played—she won! This made her the silliest dressed and world's best tennis player!

Scholastic Professional Books *More Proofreading Practice, Please! Grade 5*
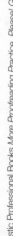

Name _____ Date _____

Dan's Fables: The Donkey and the Dog

Find and mark the twelve errors. They may be spelling, punctuation, capitalization, or grammar errors.

There once was a donkey who lived with a farmer and a dog. The donkey worked hard every day. The donkey carry bundles of sticks. It pulled the plow.

The dog, on the other hand, did very little but sleep. Each evening on the porch, the dog sat on the farmers' lap. It licked the farmer's face. The farmer scratcht the dog's ears and said, "What a good dog you is."

By and by, the donkey began to grow gealous. "Why should I work so hard?" it asked.

That day, the donkey refussed to work.

When the farmer returned home from the felds, the donkey came running. It jumped into the farmers lap, just like a dog. It tried to lick the farmer's face, just like a dog.

"Get off!" cried the farmer. You're too heavy! You'll broken my lap!"

The farmer locked the donkey in the barn. A few days later he sold the donkey to a neighbor. The neighbor worked the donkey very hard. She worked the donkey much harder than the farmer had.

"What a fool I've been," said the donkey. "now my life is much worse than it was before."

The moral of the story is . . .
Be who you is, unless you're a fool.
Then, don't be who you are.

Scholastic Professional Books *More Proofreading Practice, Please! Grade 5*

39

Name _____ Date _____

Dan's Fables: The Dog and the Donkey

Find and mark the twelve errors. They may be spelling, punctuation, capitalization, or grammar errors.

There oncet was a dog who lived with a farmer and a donkey. The dog sleep all day while the donkey worked in the fields.

"I'm tired of working," said the donkey.

"I'm tired of sleeping" said the dog.

"Let's switsh places!" they both said simultaneously.

The next morning, the donkey stayed home and slept. The dog worked. The dog pulled the wagon. It plowed the fields. The dog carried bags on it's back. As the day continued, the dog grew more and more exhosted.

The donkey slept. The donkey yawned. It swished flies with its tail. The donkey looked in the window of the farmers house. It was only 9:30 in the morning. The donkey were bored. Sleeping all day was boring.

That evening, the donkey meet the dog at the fence. "Well, how did it go, my frend?" the donkey asked the dog.

"Let's switch back to our old roles," said the dog. "you work and I'll sleep."

"All right," said the donkey.

So the next day, the donkey worked and the dog slept.
And they continued to be this way from then on.

The moral of the story is . . .

Do not never switch places with a donkey.

Scholastic Professional Books *More Proofreading Practice, Please!* Grade 5

Name _____ Date _____

Great Sports Records:
The Benny Bragan Story

Find and mark the twelve errors. They may be spelling, punctuation, capitalization, or grammar errors.

There were two outs in the ninth inning. Benny Bragan was sitting on the bench. His team was loosing by a score of 19 to 0. But Benny Bragan wasnt' no loser. He was knocking on the door of one of baseball's greatest all-time records: *the number of fidgets in one game.*

The orriginall record had been set by Old Hoss Mueller back in 1931. But Old Hoss had a big avantage. Players wore itchy wool uniforms back then, even on hot summer days. No wonder players squirmed and fidgeted so much.

Benny had the misfortune of playing in an era when players wore Cotton uniforms. Yet here it was, the ninth inning, and bragan had fidgeted 106 times already—that's over eleven fidgets per inning!

As the pitcher went into his wind-up, Benny suddenly heard a noise. It were thunder. A rain cloud appeared. Soon, the field was soaked with rain.

Benny Bragan was one fidget short of the all-time record.

One fidget!

Did Benny Bragan have any regrets.

"Not really," said Benny after the game. "The important thing is that I tried. I squirmed and fidgeted as best I could. I gave it my all. I has no regrets."

Benny Bragan are a sports heroe we can only aspire to be!

Scholastic Professional Books *More Proofreading Practice, Please! Grade 5*

41

Name _____ Date _____

Can a Horse be Elected President of the United States?

Find and mark the twelve errors. They may be spelling, punctuation, capitalization, or grammar errors.

Recently the idea of electing a horse president, of the United States has come up for consideration. Consider these points based on the U.S. Constitution.

Horses is natural born citisens. The Constitution says that the president must be a Natural born Citizen. That's what horses is, except for those that were born in foreign countries. But, you wouldn't expect them to run for president.

Horses are honest. Have you ever met a dishhonest horse? A horse would make a good president because horses never lie.

Horses don't take special interest money. Huemans can be bribed with money. All horses want are carrots and sugar cubes. This makes them harder to bribe.

Horses know what it's like to be ridden on and controlled by the rider. They has learned that they don't always get things their own way.

Horses are good at balancing the budget. Okay, so here's one thing that isn't true. Horses probably ain't very good at budgets. But otherwise; they'd make good presidents.

Let's ellect a horse soon!

Scholastic Professional Books *More Proofreading Practice, Please! Grade 5*

Superheroes You've Never Heard Of, page 7

Pizza-Eating Girl

She can eat pizza with anything on it—*anything!* You want ice cream and raisins on your pizza? She can eat it! How about a pizza with lemon drops and celery? She can eat it! Her skills come in handy when villains try to force the heroes to eat unpleasant pizza combinations.

Dictionary Man

He can look up words in the dictionary faster than any other living human being. His powers are useful for fighting against villains who use really big words.

Worm Woman

She lives underground. She can communicate with worms; not that worms have much to say. She often ends up stuck on the sidewalk in the hot sun after a rainy day.

Bargain Man

He can buy anything for the lowest possible price. This is especially helpful when other superheroes need to buy tights and uniforms. He always finds a bargain!

Gesundheit Woman

With her super hearing, she can hear people sneezing miles away. Her powers come in handy when bad guys are hiding in corners and they sneeze.

Money: It's Better Than Ever!, page 8

The U.S. Mint makes money every day. Did you know that today's money is better then ever? To see why, keep reading.

Money is 100% all natural! That's right. There are no artificial ingredients in U.S. money. Your dollars are as pure and natural as a tall redwood tree!

Money goes everywhere! Going to the beach? Take some money. Taking a vacation? Try taking money with you. Making a business deal? You'll find that money comes in handy!

Money comes in great sizes and styles! Do you like paper money or coins? Big amounts or small? Green or silver? No matter what your needs, we've got the money for you. In the styles and sizes that fit your active lifestyle.

Money has lots of uses! Want to buy something? Buy it with money. You can buy almost anything with money, including shoelaces, cinnamon rolls, hairbrushes, and even Super Bowl tickets (if you can get them).

Is Nothing Funny?, page 9

"On the subject of humor and comedy," Said Professor Mary Francis Pfaff, "Nothing can ever be *proven* to be funny So there's no real reason to laugh!"

"Laughter has no real purpose," Said the famous doctor of grins. "It's just a nervous habit we have Like fish that wiggle their fins."

"The data is clear," the professor said. "In my research, I've found There's just no point in opening your mouth And making a 'Ha ha!' sound."

Just then a tiny inchworm Hanging by its miniature toes Dropped down from the ceiling above Right on the tip of my nose!

When the professor seemed to chuckle, I said, "Excuse me, Professor Pfaff, Didn't you say that *nothing's* funny? There's *never* a reason to laugh?"

"Well," replied the professor. "I'll admit one thing is true. It *can* be funny when an inchworm lands— At least when it lands on you!"

Official Fan Club News for Matt Head, Professional Wrestler, page 10

Keeping Track of Matt

Though he had no wrestling matches this week, Matt Head was very busy. These are some of the things he accomplished this week.

- He drooled.
- He got into an argument with a tree.
- He put his tights on backwards.

Fan Club Poll

We asked you to answer the question: *What does Matt Head remind you of most?* Here are the results.

- A floor mat—14%
- A big head without a brain—62%
- A wrestling mat with no brains who argues with trees—24%

Matt Head's Diet Plan

- Breakfast: 14-ounce box of corn flakes, including the box, and 2 gallons of milk
- Light Lunch: pasta, salad, and metal screws
- Power Dinner: raw leather with radiator fluid sauce

Contest Results

Here are the results of our contest, "Why I don't want to spend the day with Matt Head." We only received one entry. Here it is.

I don't want to spend the day with Matt Head. I certainly hope I don't win this contest. —Jason Dorf

Stories Behind Inventions That Changed The World, page 11

The Jacket Zipper

The first zipper, the Model 100-A, was made of solid wood and weighed over 17 pounds. Over time, the size decreased. Metal replaced wood. A solid gold zipper weighed in at only 4.1 ounces. Unfortunately, it cost over $1,500. Finally, the Model 100-Z came out. It was a lot like the zipper of today—except two people were required to zip it up.

The Bookmark

Ted E. Bear, in a 1997 interview, disclosed, "I kept losing my place in the book I was reading. I tried putting a piece of cheese in there, but it was greasy. I tried a giant rock. It was too heavy and awkward. I tried a $100 bill. It worked well, but that was all the money I had! Finally, I tried a small slip of paper. At last, the bookmark was born!"

The Cereal Spoon

First, people tried to eat cereal with their hands. What a mess! There was milk dripping from everyone's elbows. Next, a garden shovel was tried. Too big! It was replaced with a fork. The size was good, but it leaked. Finally, someone pulled out a spoon. There was little chance after so many failures that it would work. But, it was perfect!

Celebrity Auction, page 12

These items will be offered at the Annual Celebrity Auction.

Item #406B: Hair clippings from country singer Milt Hayseed. Milt gets a haircut every week. His barber collects the clippings. Bidding starts at $50 a bunch. Each bunch contains forty or more strands.

Item #418C: Peanut butter sandwich not eaten by child superstar Spencer Twirp When Spencer was on his cross-country tour, one of his assistants ordered a sandwich for him. "I hate peanut butter!" cried Spencer. This is the very sandwich that Spencer never touched. Bidding starts at $1,200.

Item #423A: Elevator button pushed by movie superstar Tanya Ruffage When Tanya made the classic film *Dripless*, she stayed on the eleventh floor of the Park Boulevard Hotel. This is the elevator button she pushed to get to that floor. Bidding starts at $13,000.

Item #511D: Towel used by sports star Manny Meshooga During the 2002 semi-finals, a fan gave Manny this towel to autograph. Manny didn't sign it, but he did wipe his shoes on the towel. Bidding starts at $5,000.

Scholastic Professional Books *More Proofreading Practice, Please! Grade 5*

43

Answer Key

The World's Dullest Videos, page 13

Do you love dull videos? Then this is the collection for you. For only $39.95 per month we'll deliver a video to your door. The selections include these titles.

Water Boiling

This classic shows the entire process, from start to finish. Watch as the pot is filled with water. See the heat being turned on! Then wait for the water to boil. It seems like it takes forever!

Grass Growing

Are you an outdoor-type person? Do you love nature? This fabulous 24-part video is for you. Watch as, at first, nothing seems to happen. But then as the hours (and days!) pass, a change occurs. Isn't the grass a tiny bit longer than it was at the begining? Watch for the sequel, *Mowing*.

The Stone

This is the video for true rock fans. No scenery. No talk. No music. Just a camera focused on a common stone for six solid hours. Nothing happens. Nothing changes. By far, this is the dullest video in our collection!

If I Had Three Wishes, Here's What I'd Do, page 14

If I had three wishes, here's what I'd do:
I'd use my first wish (which would leave me just two)
And wish for three wishes—that would make five,
Which would make me the luckyest person alive!

Because after that, I could wish again,
And keep on going until I'd passed ten.
Then I'd keep wishing until I had a bunch,
Then I'd stop, take a break, and wish for something good
for lunch.

After lunch I'd wish more and pile up the wishes—
Eleven, twelve, but not thirteen (you see, I'm superstitious).

After I had a hundred wishes, I think I'd take a break.
I wouldn't want to get tired and make a foolish mistake.
If I had a *thousand* wishes, maybe that'd be enough,
Or maybe I'd keep going, and wish for yet more stuff.
After a *million* wishes, I guess I'd need no more.
So then I'd start wishing for ideas of things
To use my million wishes for.

How to Get Rid of Common Yard Pests, page 15

Michael, the five-year-old pest who tramples your rose bushes

Young children are drawn to the sound of bells. Get a bell that sounds just like the one on your local ice cream truck. Go arond to the front of the house and ring the bell. Close the gate after he leaves.

Ms. Peeve, the door-to-door salesperson

Tell Ms. Peeve that you can't talk right now. But you'd like to talk later by telephone. Ask for Ms. Peeve's home phone number. This should frighten her away for good.

Steve, the teenage pest

Teenagers don't like corny music. Get a recording of some really lame music. Turn the volume up loud. This should get rid of Steve in no time.

Bonnie, the cat who hides under your porch

Cats are drawn to the sound of a can opening. Go out in the front yard, well away from the affected area. Open a can of something that cats don't like, like spinach or green beans. Bonnie will come running. But she'll be so disappointed that she won't come back again.

My Most Embarrassing Moment, page 16

This is *so* embarrassing that I can barely talk about it. Let me start by telling you a little bit about myself. I'm a spider. My name is Lulu. I live in a web that I spin each and every day. It's in the attic of a building on eighth street. I picked this location because I have eight legs. I think I eat insects. That may sound yucky to you. I think they are delicious.

One more thing. I've got poisonous fangs. I could bring down an elephant if I needed to. But I prefer insects.

This is my embarrassing moment. I was sitting in my web in the attic of 1818 Eighth Street, Hartford, connecticut. I heard a rustling. "Aha!" I thought. "Lunch!" I heard some struggling and a muffled cry for help. So I rushed over to the noise. I wrapped the victim up in silk. I was just about to inject my poison when I heard a voice cry "It's me! Walter!"

"Walter?" I thought. It wasn't an insect at all. It was an arachnid, like me. In fact, it was Walter the Spider, my boyfriend! I had caught him in my web! I had even wrapped him up.

I was so embarrassed I thought I'd never live it down. Walter forgave me. and we played on swings made of silk that Walter hung from my web.

The Really Loud Noise Show, page 17

Good evening. I'm Bob Drumm. Welcome to "the Really Loud Noise Show." Each week on "The Really Loud Noise Show," we bring you the loudest noise we can find. We'll start off today with a really loud train going 80 miles per hour.

Next, we add the trains whistle.

We follow the train noises with the noon ringing of bells in a nearby church.

The next thing you hear will be the sound heard if you were parked across the street from the church in a car with huge stereo speakers blaring loud music while your passenger is beating a garbage can with a hammer. Meanwhile, a dog is sitting in the backseat and is barking furiously at a mail carrier who is passing by.

For our final loud noise of the evening, the railroad tracks are next to a school playground where one hundred screaming kindergarten students have just started to play. Of course, an ice cream truck has just pulled up.

Now that's some loud noise! See you next week, everyone! What? You can't hear me? I'd better speak *louder*!

Left Brain/Right Brain, page 18

Your brain has a left side and a right side. Each side is specialized for different tasks.

Your left brain is good for arguing, counting money, thinking of excuses, making hasty decisions, changing TV channels, and thinking of someone to blame when something goes wrong.

Your right brain is good for arranging furniture, jumping to conclusions, getting mad when something goes wrong, finding lost socks, and remembering where things are in the refrigerator.

How do your two brains work together to solve a problem? Read the following problem to find out.

Two trains leave their stations at exactly 12 noon. One is traveling at 80 miles per hour from Baltimore to Pittsburgh. The other is traveling at 63 miles per hour from Pittsburgh to baltimore. How much is the lunch special on the second train?

Your left brain springs into action first, thinking, "I can't solve this problem in a million years. I can't solve this problem, either."

Then your right brain contributes, "I can't solve this problem, either."

Now your left brain takes control, thinking, "I give up. There's no point in trying."

Finally your right brain finishes the task, thinking, "I'm hungry. I'll make a peanut butter sandwich."

Scholastic Professional Books *More Proofreading Practice, Please!* Grade 5

Teen Beat Magazine Interview: The Four Whiners, page 19

TEEN BEAT: Welcome. We're interviewing this month's hottest new band—The Four whiners.
WHINERS: Hi.
TEEN BEAT: Why don't you introduce yourselves?
GUMBY: I'm Gumby Carlson. I do the lead lip-synching.
WEASEL: I'm Weasel Whitney. I just stand on stage.
CINDY: I'm Cindy Cruz from a Ranch in Montana. I make my lips pout. See?
MONICA: I'm Monica Silver. I hum. Then everyone always tells me to be quiet.
TEEN BEAT: Tell us about your new CD called "The Cheese songs."
GUMBY: We haven't really heard it yet.
TEEN BEAT: Don't you know what's on it?
CINDY: You have to understand. First, real Musicians play the music.
WEASEL: Then good singers sing the songs.
MONICA: Then dancers are filmed for the videos.
TEEN BEAT: What do you actually do?
WEASEL: We sort of hang around backstage and play card games.
TEEN BEAT: Is it true that, except for your photograph on the cover, you really had no part in the making of your own hit CD?
GUMBY: (taking off his mask) Actually, we wear masks.
TEEN BEAT: (shocked) Oh, my goodness!
MONICA: (shrugs) Would you like our autographs?

Beach Teens, page 22

The following is the script for the new hit TV show starring Jason Goozle and Jennie Fibb.
Jennie: Jason, I can't go with you to the Thanksgiving Dance.
Jason: Why not? Is it because I'm dull unpopular, and have a bad haircut?
Jennie: No, it's not that.
Jason: Is it because I'm rude, I mumble, and I never stop talking about myself?
Jennie: No, it's not that, either.
Jason: Then what is it Jennie? Is it because all of your friends hate me? Plus, I eat dog food? And I haven't taken a bath in over six months? Do you hold those things against me, Jennie?
Jennie: No, Jason, I don't. I don't know how to say this.
Jason: Go ahead and say it, Jennie. I can take it.
Jennie: There's not going to be a Thanksgiving Dance, Jason.
Jason: Was it cancelled?
Jennie: No, it wasn't cancelled. There isn't any dance. There never was any dance. It's not even Thanksgiving, Jason. It's july. You can't have a Thanksgiving Dance in July.
Jason: So, does that mean you won't be going with me?
Jennie: No, I won't.
Jason: One more thing, Jennie. Suppose it were Thanksgiving, and suppose there were a Thanksgiving Dance. Would you have gone with me?
Jennie: Not a chance, Jason.
Jason: Thought so.

FAQ.com, page 20

Welcome to FAQ.com. FAQ stands for Frequently Asked Questions. FAQ.com attempts to answer questions about those questions.

Question: What's your most frequently asked question?
Answer: The most frequently asked question is, "What is your most frequently asked question?"

Question: Isn't that what I just asked?
Answer: No, you asked, "What's your most frequently asked question?" We answered "The most frequently asked question is, 'What is your most frequently asked question?'"

Question: Why am I so confused?
Answer: That's the second-most frequently asked question. The answer is, "Because the answer to your first question was so confusing, you're still confused."

Question: So what should I do?
Answer: We suggest that you go to Confused.com. This site gives answers to people who have become confused after visiting our site. Good Luck.

Weird Spell 2002, page 23

Juan: Welcome to "Weird Spell 2002." It's the game where players compete to see who can spell words in the weirdest way. I'm Juan Bost, your host. And now, let's hear from our first weird speller.
Donna: My name is Donna pike. I'm a really weird speller. One time I spelled cat without a c, an a, or a t!
Juan: Wow! Here's your first word, Donna. Spell fishes.
Donna: That would be "p-h-i-c-i-o-u-s."
Juan: That's really weird, Donna. How do you explain it?
Donna: The ph makes an "F" sound in the word phonograph.
Juan: Oh, that's clever.
Donna: Then the end of the word is just like the end of suspicious.
Juan: That's clever, Donna. That sure is a weird way to spell a word.
Donna: Thank you very much. What do I win?
Juan: You win a million dollars! sorry, did I say "million"? I meant to say, "you win the ten-dollar prize!"
Donna: Well, thanks anyway.
Juan: That's all the time we have now for "Weird Spell 2002" —the game where players spell words in weird ways.

The Case of the Mummy's Gold, page 21

Hello, I'm Lucy Luck. I'm a private eye. I was sitting in my office when Dr. Jane Hanks, the famous Explorer, walked in. A couple of years ago, Dr. Hanks found the famous Mummy's Gold. However, the gold had been stolen from her and she'd been searching for it ever since.
"Look at this letter," Dr. Hanks said. The letter contained a map of what looked like the Gobi desert. "I traveled to Mongolia in asia and searched everywhere in the southeast corner of the Gobi Desert. I didn't find the Gold."
"Are you hungry, Dr. Hanks?" I asked. "Let's go eat dinner." I took her to a dark and distant neighborhood. We walked into a little restaurant called gobi's.
"Surely," she said, "you don't think—"
I went to a small table in the southeast corner of the restaurant. A sign said, "Dessert." I looked under the table. There was a large chest filled with the Mummy's Gold!
"You found it!" cried Dr. Hanks. "How can I ever thank you?"
"It's no big deal," I said, even though I knew it was.
"I just have one question," said Dr. Hanks as we hauled the chest out. "I looked at the map. It says Desert, not Dessert. It's clear as a bell."
"Hey," I said. "People make mistakes."
"They sure do," said Dr. Hanks.

Classic Warning Labels, page 24

Warning on Shoes
The soles on these shoes are made of Rubber. In the event that you are attacked by a group of rubber-eating space aliens, take off shoes. Do not leave a trail of erasers for them to follow!

Warning on Alligator Exhibit
Please refrain from jumping over the fence, swimming the moat, scaling the wall, and poking the alligators with a stick. Do not say "You can't hurt me a bit!" Alligators can hurt you a bit.

Warning on Movie Poster
This film is rated EP. (Extremely Pointless). please do not try to analyze the plot, understand the characters, or figure out what happens in the end. For the most part, this movie does not make any sense.

Warning on Tomato Sauce Can
Tomato sauce is not intended to be poured on cornflakes, in hair, or in fish bowls. People who pour it in their hair may develop symptoms of Tomato Sauce hair Condition. This condition includes hair that smells like tomato sauce and that could be eaten if somebody is foolish enough to try it.

Scholastic Professional Books More Proofreading Practice, Please! Grade 5

45

Answer Key

Danny the K, Proofreader for the Stars, page 25

My name is Danny the K. I don't like to brag, but I'm probably the greatest proofreader of all time. I've proofread for presidents, kings, pop stars, quarterbacks, and movie tycoons.

I'll never forget the day the president called me up. "Danny," he said. "You've got to proofread my speech. I'll give you the Medal Of Honor. I'll name a street after you. Just tell me what you want. I'll do it."

"Hold on a second, Mr. President," I said. "I don't want a Medal of Honor. I don't want a street. I'm just a proofreader. I just want to do my job."

"You are right," said the president. "I'm sorry." I proofread the speech for him. Wouldn't you know it? That was the finest speech he ever made!

Then there was the time my favorite actor, Marva Marvelous, called me. "Darling," she said. "You just must proofread my new script. If you did, I'll give you anything. I'll give you a million dollars."

"Hold on a second there, Marva," I said. "I'm just a proofreader, not a movie star. I can't take a million dollars for that."

"Why not?" Marva asked.

"Because I want two million dollars," I said.

Now two million dollars may seem to be a ridiculous amount for someone to pay for proofreading. But, I proofread this piece and you can see what a greatest job I did!

Pensington-400 Toasting System, page 26

Congratulations! You're the proud new owner of the Pensington-400 Toasting System.

Before You Toast

Make sure that you have the proper equipment. You will need the Pensington-400, bread, butter, a knife, safety goggles and helmet, and a plate.

Safety Precautions

Always wear your safety goggles and helmet when using the toaster. When properly handled, toast is 100% safe. Beware of high-speed toast particles that break off from the main bread slice while buttering. These particles can travel at speeds up to 125 miles per hour.

Troubleshooting

Problem: My helmet came unsnapped while I was buttering. What should I do?

Solution: Stop buttering immediately. With your left hand, stabilize the toast. When you are sure the toast is safe, use your right hand to snap your helmet. Once your helmet is secure, resume buttering.

Problem: I was making toast when I heard sirens. Firefighters broke down my front door. What happened?

Solution: You may have burned your toast. Is it covered with flames? Do the flames reach halfway to the ceiling? If so, then read page 54, "How to survive a burnt toast emergency."

The Pegwegger Fashion Collection, page 27

Marvelous Muffin Mittens

While traveling in a rural area of upper Scotland, I noticed the locals wearing marvelous mittens. I said to Roland, my assistant, "You and I need pairs of those mittens." It seems the people were wearing special kinds of muffins shaped like mittens. Now the new Pegwegger Collection offers "Muffin Mittens." Of course, if you get hungry, you can eat your mittens!

Bus Boy Slacks

Have you noticed how great café bus boys look? That's because they spill food on their pants. The "café bus boy look" has inspired fabulous pants. Be cautious, don't wear the pants near hungry dogs!

Tissue Box Shoes

I was lying by the pool in Pango Pango when I noticed that I'd left my comfortable shoes inside my hotel room. What was I to do? I put two tissue boxes and putted them on my feet. Like all great ideas, the Tissue Box Shoes came from this event. Furthermore, I wore the Tissue Box Shoes in a soccer game and scored three goals!

The Secrets of the Great Decepto, page 28

The Saw-the-Assistant-in-Half Trick

First, I put my assistant in a box. Next, I wave a curtain over the box. Then, I saw the box in half. Finally, I put the two back together. When my assistant gets up, the audience applauds.

How it's done: When I pull the curtain over the box I run backstage. I am quickly replaced by a real magician who knows how to do the trick. I stand backstage until the trick is over. I run back at the end as the audience applauds.

The Pull-a-Rabbit-Out-of-a-Hat Trick

First, I show the audience a hat. There is nothing inside. Next, I put on the hat. Then, I wave my hand and take off the hat. When a rabbit jumps out, the audience applauds.

How it's done: When I wave my hand, I'm actually giving the signal for a rabbit to run onto the stage. This rabbit is a licensed magician and knows how to perform the trick flawlessly. When the trick is over, the audience applauds.

The Float-the-Assistant-Above-the-Stage Illusion

First, my assistant lies down. Next, I pass my cape over her. Then, she begins to float. I pass hoops around her to show that she is not being held by wires. The audience applauds.

How it's done: When I pass my cape over my assistant, a flock of trained hummingbirds flies on the stage and lifts her in the air. They hover in the air while I pass hoops to show that there are no wires. When the hummingbirds leave, my assistant stands up and the audience applauds.

What They Do on Their Days Off, page 29

Centipede

On my day off, I try to stay off my feet. I have one hundred of them, you know. Sometimes my brother and me go shopping for shoes. That's not easy when you each need fifty pairs!

Toll Booth Collector

I love collecting tolls. I set up a table on my street. I collect tolls from bigger cars, small trucks, and even children on tricycles. Don't worry, I always give the money back!

Clown

I like to go shopping for clown equipment. Do you know how hard it is to find clown shoes? Or, have you ever shopped for glow-in-the-dark orange hair? Also, I like to practice squirting people with lapel flowers.

House Fly

I sometimes sit on a window blind for about twelve hours and do nothing. Most of the time, I like making a pest of myself. Hey, when you're a fly, that's what you do!

Billionaire

I like to count money. I empty all the change from the pockets of my hundreds of suits. I pulled the coins from my penny loafers. I like to make stacks of coins and bills on my dining room table. My favorite hobby is counting and this gives me a chance to practice it.

The Boy Who Cried "Wulf!", page 30

There once was a smaller car company named Wulf whose cars were not selling well.

The Big Boss was frustrated. She hired a boy to sit by the road and look at the cars that went by.

"You sit right here," she told the boy. "Every time you see a Wulf drive by I want you to cry 'Wulf!'"

The boy did as he was told. Each time a Wulf drove by he cried, "Wulf!"

This might have been the end of the story were it not for a real wolf that happened to come by.

The boy cried, "Wulf!" when he saw the real wolf. But, no one paid any attention.

"I mean it!" he repeated. "It is a wolf!" Again, no one paid any attention.

So when the real wolf came to where the Big Boss was sitting, she and the Wulf sales force panicked and ran. The wolf stayed and ate all of the food on the buffet table.

In the end, the boy stayed on the job until many years later when he took over as Big Boss.

The moral of the story is . . .

Never cry wulf when it's really a wolf!

Scholastic Professional Books *More Proofreading Practice, Please!* Grade 5

True Confessions: I Abandoned My Children!, page 31

I still can't believe it. I always thought I'd be a good mother, but something came over me. I still don't know what.

I should say a little about myself. I was born in a large pond. I come from a biggest family. There were 4,000 in my family. That's 2,000 girls and 2,000 boys. We were the biggest family in the pond.

My mother left us. We were only young tadpoles, but we were on our own. I remember thinking, *When I have kids, it won't be like this.*

But then, sure enough, I laid about 5,000 eggs. I was determined to treat each and every one of them like an individual.

Then something came over me. Suddenly, I just hopped up and left. I got on the Internet and looked up frog behavior. No wonder I let my tadpoles go!

Epilog

I was surprised and proud at how good my children all turned out. Thousands made it. They are good croakers. They grew up tall and straight and green. Just like me!

Behind the Special Effects in Today's Hit Movies, page 32

Dear State-of-the-Art,

Recently, I saw the movie *Detonation*, starring Arnold Morphus. It had a lot of great special effect. But, the part I liked best came near the end. There were no car chases, and not even any space aliens in the scene. The two characters were just talking. How did they do that?
Signed, Curious

Dear Curious,

The part of the movie that you liked is called *acting.* Acting requires that the stars act, talk, and make gestures just like real people. Though acting in today's movies is quite rare, believe it or not, in the olden days, acting was actually quite common in movies!
Signed, State-of-the-Art

Dear State-of-the-Art,
How did they make the four cockroaches speak their lines in the movie *Roach Motel?*
Signed, PUZZLED

Dear Puzzled,
This is an easy one! They just held up cue cards. The roaches read their lines right off the cue cards.
Signed, State-of-the-Art

Jenny Bosco, Olympic Swimmer, and Her Cat Ruffles, page 33

My name is Jenny Bosco. I'm an Olympic swimmer. I swim in the 50-yard free-style dog paddle. I always thought that Ruffles, my best friend, would be there beside me.

On the first day of training, I notice something was wrong. I jumped in the pool, but Ruffles didn't follow me.

I took her to seven different specialists. They all came to the same conclusion: *Cats don't like water.*

So each day, I would swim laps. Ruffles would sit by the pool reading the newspaper. But, Ruffles seemed restless.

Then I heard more bad news. I took Ruffles to the eye doctor. He tell me that *cats can't read.*

Once again, I was crushed. I thought, *I'll win a gold medal in the Olympics anyway.*

Well, I didn't win a gold medal. In fact, I missed the whole competition. On the day of the race, I overslept and was disqualified. Ruffles's watch had stopped!

I swam anyway. It was during the *diving* competition. I was almost hit by someone doing a two-and-one-half-full-twisting gainer. But as the police escorted me away, I thought about Ruffles. She may hate water. She may never learn to read. But, she still is my best friend. I think she and I will go out for the three-legged race next Olympics.

Are You Jealous?, page 34

Bert: Welcome to the quiz show, "Are You Jealous?" I'm Bert Envy, your host. Our first contestant is Edna Fingers. Edna, here are your first question. *Suppose your best friend Jasper gets a new puppy for his birthday. Are you jealous?*
Edna: No, Bert, I'm not.
Bert: Correct for 50 points! And what's your reason, Edna?
Edna: I have my own puppy, Bert. Plus, my puppy doesn't chew or shoes the way Jasper's puppy does.
Bert: Very nice, Edna, here's your second question. *Suppose Jasper get invited to go over to Scooter's house to play and you don't get to go. Are you jealous?*
Edna: No, I'm not, Bert. I'll tell you why. I don't like to go over to Scooter's and play with his video games. I'd rather stay here by myself.
Bert: And that is correct for 100 points! Now here's your final question, Edna. *Your friend Jasper gets to be on the TV show "Who wants a Sandwich?" Are you jealous?*
Edna: No, I'm not Bert, because I'm currently appearing on a TV show.
Bert: "Who Wants a Sandwich?" is a more popular show than "Are You Jealous?" So, you're *incorrect*, Edna. You *should* be jealous. That's minus 150 points! Which brings your score to zero, goose egg, nothing.
Edna: Bye, Bert. I'm going to try out for "Who Wants a Sandwich?"
Bert: That's all the time we have now. See you next time!

A Statement From Class President Mona Turpin, page 35

My fellow classmates, as president of our class, I know that you have put your trust in me. You trusted me when you elected me president. You trusted me when we passed the recess rule that increased the length of recess by over 15 percent. You trusted me when I asked for your support on the candy ban.

At that time, I explained how I felt. Candy is bad for you. It rots your teeth. It's expensive. Basically, it has no place in our school.

When we passed the candy ban, I felt proud. I felt we had done something for all of the students of webster School. I still feel that way.

Recently though, some troubling events have come to light. Candy wrappers were found in my locker. My book bag was described as "smelling like chocolate." I'd like to tell you that these accusations are a mistake. I'd like to say that I didn't bring candy to school. I'd like to say that I didn't eat it secretly in the Student Council Room, stuffing it into my mouth as fast as I could.

But if I told you these things, I'd be lying. All I can tell you is that I am sorry. What did I learn from this experience? I learned about honesty. I learned about responsibility. I learned that it's easier to talk the talk than to walk the walk. I learned all of these things. But most of all, I learned something about myself.

I learned that I *really* like candy.

Ask Dr. Science, page 36

Question: How do we know that Earth goes around the sun?
Dr. Science: It's obvious that Earth goes around something. Is it a telephone pole? Is it a raccoon? If you look closely in a science book you will see a diagram with a tiny Earth traveling around the sun—not around a telephone pole or a raccoon.

Question: What is photosynthesis?
Dr. Science: Photosynthesis is what happens when someone is taking a picture and you look the other way. Then you get the photograph back and you look really stupid. Then you say, "Photosynthesis caused that to happen."

Question: How does a computer work?
Dr. Science: There are three ways to make a computer work. First, plug it in. Second, turn it on. And third, say out loud, "Why won't this thing work?"

Question: Why do birds fly south?
Dr. Science: Birds are looking for coins on the ground. They fly a little bit. Then they fly a little bit more. Pretty soon, they end up in Florida.

Answer Key

Wrong Number!, page 37

The following is some of the most outrageously wrong (cap) numbers ever dialed. This first call came to the house of Mr. Rudy Remo of Baltimore, maryland. Listen closely.

Caller: Hello, who's this?

Rudy: No, who is this?

Caller: I was trying to call 555-3221.

Rudy: This is 555-9928. You're not even close!

Caller: Wow! You're right. I'm sorry. I really am.

Rudy: That's okay. It could happen to anyone.

But could it happen to anyone? Listen to what happens next at the Remo household.

Rudy: Hello, is Erica there?

Caller: There is no Erica here. What number are you trying to reach?

Caller: I am trying to reach 555-3221.

Rudy: Well, you're off by a mile. This is 555-9928. Say, didn't you just call a few minutes ago?

Caller: (disguising his voice) Who, me? No, it must have been someone else.

There you have it—a number so wrong that we had our experts analyze the last four digits. Do you know what they found? Every digit was wrong! Not a single digit was correct! Now, how's that for a shocking event?

Great Sports Records: The Tanya Macarena Story, page 38

"Winning a match is great," said tennis legend Tanya Macarena. "But do you know what's more important than winning? What I wear on the court. That's what it's really all about."

It wasn't always like this for Tanya Macarena. At one point she was satisfied just winning matches. And, as the top player in the world, she won a lot of matches.

"But something was missing," revealed Tanya. "I would win my match, but then I would look over and see that my opponents outfit was sillier than mine. This bothered me."

So Tanya hired Minnie Vulch to design her tennis outfits. Ms. Vulch said, "I don't know anything about fashion. You'll be able to tell by my designs."

Over time, Ms. Vulch helped design dozens of new outfits for Tanya. Each one was sillier than the last.

"At first, my outfits were silly, but not really ridiculous," said Tanya. "The real breakthrough came at the U.S. Open. I wore what can be described as a clown suit."

"I was amazed she could play with those big floppy shoes and the red rubber nose," confessed Minnie.

But Tanya not only played—she won! This made her the silliest dressed and world's best tennis player!

Dan's Fables: The Donkey and the Dog, page 39

There once was a donkey who lived with a farmer and a dog. The donkey worked hard every day. The donkey carried bundles of sticks. It pulled the plow.

The dog, on the other hand, did very little but sleep. Each evening on the porch, the dog sat on the farmer's lap. It licked the farmer's face. The farmer scratched the dog's ears and said, "What a good dog you are."

By and by, the donkey began to grow jealous. "Why should I work so hard?" it asked.

That day, the donkey refused to work.

When the farmer returned home from the fields, the donkey came running. It jumped into the farmer's lap, just like a dog. It tried to lick the farmer's face, just like a dog.

"Get off!" cried the farmer. "You're too heavy! You'll break my lap!"

The farmer locked the donkey in the barn. A few days later he sold the donkey to a neighbor. The neighbor worked the donkey very hard. She worked the donkey much harder than the farmer had.

"What a fool I've been," said the donkey, "now my life is much worse than it was before."

The moral of the story is . . . Be who you are, unless you're a fool. Then, don't be who you are.

Dan's Fables: The Dog and the Donkey, page 40

There once was a dog who lived with a farmer and a donkey. The dog slept all day while the donkey worked in the fields.

"I'm tired of working," said the donkey.

"I'm tired of sleeping," said the dog.

"Let's switch places!" they both said simultaneously.

The next morning, the donkey stayed home and slept. The dog worked. The dog pulled the wagon. It plowed the fields. The dog carried bags on its back. As the day continued, the dog grew more and more exhausted.

The donkey slept. The donkey yawned. It swished flies with its tail. The donkey looked in the window of the farmer's house. It was only 9:30 in the morning. The donkey was bored. Sleeping all day was boring.

That evening, the donkey met the dog at the fence.

"Well, how did it go, my friend?" the donkey asked the dog.

"Let's switch back to our old roles," said the dog, "you work and I'll sleep."

"All right," said the donkey.

So the next day, the donkey worked and the dog slept. And they continued to be this way from then on.

The moral of the story is . . .

Do not ever switch places with a donkey.

Great Sports Records: The Benny Bragan Story, page 41

There were two outs in the ninth inning. Benny Bragan was sitting on the bench. His team was losing by a score of 19 to 0. But Benny Bragan wasn't a loser. He was knocking on the door of one of baseball's greatest all-time records: the number of fidgets in one game.

The original record had been set by Old Hoss Mueller back in 1931. But Old Hoss had a big advantage. Players wore itchy wool uniforms back then, even on hot summer days. No wonder players squirmed and fidgeted so much.

Benny had the misfortune of playing in an era when players wore cotton uniforms. Yet here it was, the ninth inning, and Bragan had fidgeted 106 times already—that's over eleven fidgets per inning!

As the pitcher went into his wind-up, Benny suddenly heard a noise. It was thunder. A rain cloud appeared. Soon, the field was soaked with rain.

Benny Bragan was one fidget short of the all-time record. One fidget!

Did Benny Bragan have any regrets?

"Not really," said Benny after the game. "The important thing is that I tried. I squirmed and fidgeted as best I could. I gave it my all. I have no regrets."

Benny Bragan is a sports hero we can only aspire to be!

Can a Horse be Elected President of the United States?, page 42

Recently the idea of electing a horse president of the United States has come up for consideration. Consider these points based on the U.S. Constitution.

Horses are natural born citizens. The Constitution says that the president must be a natural born citizen. That's what horses are, except for those that were born in foreign countries. But, you wouldn't expect them to run for president.

Horses are honest. Have you ever met a dishonest horse? A horse would make a good president because horses never lie.

Horses don't take special interest money. Humans can be bribed with money. All horses want are carrots and sugar cubes. This makes them harder to bribe.

Horses know what it's like to be ridden on and controlled by the rider. They have learned that they don't always get things their own way.

Horses are good at balancing the budget. Okay, so here's one thing that isn't true. Horses probably aren't very good at budgets. But otherwise, they'd make good presidents.

Let's elect a horse soon

Scholastic Professional Books More Proofreading Practice, Please! Grade 5